TOO-GOOD-TO-BE-TRUE SHOES

PAUL SHIPTON

Illustrated by Judy Brown

PACIFIC
L E A R N I N G

This Americanized Edition of *Too-Good-to-Be-True Shoes,*
originally published in English in 1996, is published by
arrangement with Oxford University Press.

05 04 03 02 01
10 9 8 7 6 5 4 3 2 1

Published by
Pacific Learning
P.O. Box 2723
Huntington Beach, CA 92647-0723
www.pacificlearning.com

ISBN: 1-59055-036-6
PL-7406

Contents

The Perfect Shoes

Jake couldn't believe it when he saw
them. The running shoes were just
sitting on top of a cardboard box, next
to a bunch of trash cans.

Anna was busy telling him the plot
of some science-fiction book she was
reading, but Jake wasn't listening. He
just gazed at the shoes. They looked
expensive and brand-new.

"Look," he finally said.

Anna followed his pointing finger.

A pair of shoes... So?

Not just any pair. These are perfect!

He edged closer.

Maybe it's one of those things that people see in the desert when they're dying for water. A...

mirage?

Yeah! A mirage!

No – these were real, all right.

Jake, they're just a pair of running shoes, not buried treasure!

Anna was his best friend, but Jake didn't expect her to understand. She knew he liked running. She even helped time him when he ran around the park. Jake, however, didn't just *like* running – he was *crazy* about it.

He looked inside the shoes.

They're even my size! Why would anyone throw them away?

Anna shrugged. Jake unzipped his gym bag.

He could even hear the rumble of the garbage truck coming from down the street.

"You don't even know where they've been," Anna said in a horrified voice.

It was Jake's turn to shrug. He stuffed the shoes into his bag.

"It's the County Cross-Country Championships in two weeks," he said. "I'll never do well in my beat-up old shoes. These will give me a chance."

Anna nodded. She knew how important the championships were to Jake. Five runners were selected from each school in the county. Jake hadn't been chosen, but then Rob Curtis had to have his tonsils out. Jake was his replacement in the race.

"I'm going to try them out in the park after school. Will you come and time me?" Jake asked.

He knew what the answer would be. They might be interested in different things – he loved running, and Anna spent all her time reading about magic and aliens and stuff like that, but he knew she would help him.

Okay. Now about that book...

9

Kevin Beadle

Jake usually liked school, but that day seemed to drag on forever.

When the bell finally rang, he pelted to the locker room and got ready. The running shoes felt fantastic on his feet – almost as if they had been made for him.

He was waiting for Anna outside the school, when Kevin Beadle walked by.

"Well, well. Slowpoke Jake got some nice, new running shoes, did he?"

Beadle was the best runner in school. The problem was he *knew* it, and he never let anyone else forget it either.

"You know they won't help," Beadle said. "You could run in snazzy shoes, flip-flops, or army boots, Jake Crandall! All you'll see of me in the County Championships is a cloud of dust!"

I'd like to wipe that smirk off his face, Jake thought, but he knew he had no chance of beating Beadle. He'd be happy if he just did okay in the race. He didn't want to let himself down.

The Trial Run

Anna sat on the park bench and got her watch ready, while Jake did his warm-up stretches.

I'll do four laps today.

Anna nodded.

Okay. I'll tell you how you're doing on each.

Jake began to run. Anna glanced at her watch, then she opened her book and started reading.

Usually Jake set out at a light jog and then sped up, but today was different. He reached top speed immediately. He didn't plan it – it just happened. It felt as if he were running on air. His feet were a blur.

He had to shout at Anna so that she would look up from her book. She called out his lap time as he whizzed by. She couldn't believe he had finished one lap already.

That's your fastest ever!

The second lap was even faster. Jake zoomed around and he didn't even feel out of breath – not at all! In fact, he felt wonderful, and he was still picking up speed!

Anna had stopped reading now. She was watching in amazement.

The third lap flashed by too. This was normally the time when Jake got a stitch in his side and began to wheeze. Not today. He zoomed around the park and he still felt strong.

It almost felt as if the shoes were doing the running for him and he was just along for the ride!

Anna wasn't even checking the watch anymore. The fourth lap was the fastest of all.

Then rubber screeched on concrete as Jake came to a stop.

"That was... incredible," Anna said.

"You know, it *felt* incredible," Jake said happily.

"You aren't even out of breath," she continued.

Jake shook his head and grinned, but Anna narrowed her eyes.

I take it back. Those are pretty amazing shoes.

Jake looked down at his new running shoes. He was so excited that he didn't notice the tone in Anna's voice. It was as if she thought that something was *very, very wrong.*

Anna Figures It Out

Jake decided to keep the shoes in his
locker at school. He didn't want to
take them home.

"My mom and dad will never
believe I found them in the garbage,"
he explained. "They'll make me turn
them in to the Lost and Found."

The next day Jake decided to do six
laps around the park. Anna made sure
she was there again to watch.

Just like before, Jake set off at a blistering pace. Once again he was amazingly fast, and once again he wasn't out of breath at all. His feet flew over the ground, and he finished the first three laps in lightning speed.

This time Anna watched carefully. She knew no pair of normal running shoes could make such a difference. She tried to think of an explanation, but she couldn't.

She had read stories about things like magic rings and lanterns... but that's just what they were – *stories*. She had never heard of anything as weird as magic *running shoes!*

Suddenly a dog ran out across Jake's path. Anna tried to shout out a warning, but she was too late.

Jake didn't seem to notice the dog, but he leaped into the air. He soared high over the puzzled dog, then went on running. He finished the lap and stopped when he reached Anna.

"So how were you able to jump over it? How...?" she asked.

Understanding hit her like a bucket of cold water. It was crazy, but somehow she knew it was true.

"It's the running shoes!" she burst out. "It's as if they have a life of their own! I mean, no one could run that fast. The shoes were doing it. You were just a passenger."

Anna broke in. "Just now…
somehow the shoes 'saw' that dog.
Somehow they 'knew' to jump over it."

Anna's mind was racing. Shoes
that could think for themselves?
Magic? Aliens, maybe? They didn't
look very alien, though – they even
had MADE IN THE USA written on
the bottom.

She knelt down and stared at the shoes. "What are you?"

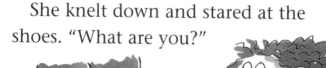

Of course, the shoes said nothing but Jake started backing up.

"Listen!" he said loudly. "I don't care what these shoes are, or where they came from! All I know is that now *I* have them and I'm going to win the County Championships!"

Anna shook her head. "*You* aren't going to be the one who will win it. Anyone could win if they wore those shoes. It proves nothing..."

Jake wouldn't listen.

"You think I should give them up, don't you?" he shouted. "Well I won't! These shoes are my only chance to win any race. I don't need to know how they do it... and I don't need any help!"

With that he turned and ran off like a speeding train.

It Proves Nothing

The day of the championships drew closer. Every day Jake went to the park to run, and every day he carefully placed the shoes back in his locker when he was done.

He just wished Anna could see how fast he was now. He felt terrible about having an argument with her. *Still*, he told himself, *Anna doesn't understand how important this is to me. I'll make up with her after the race. It's better to concentrate on winning for now.*

For it seemed certain that he would win. How could he lose?

With each practice session he was even faster. He just had to relax and the shoes did the running. He didn't even have to move his arms. He could run along eating a bag of potato chips or reading the comics, and he was still as fast as ever.

Soon it was the Friday before the big race. Jake had his final training run around the park.

When he finished he checked his watch – it was his fastest time yet.

So why didn't he feel happy about it? Anna's words echoed in his mind: "*You* aren't going to be the one who will win it... It proves nothing..."

Jake trudged back to school. He didn't notice that someone had been watching him as he ran – someone who could not believe his eyes.

This someone followed Jake all the way back to school and watched him place the running shoes in his locker... Kevin Beadle.

Jake Decides

Jake slept badly, but in the morning things seemed clear. He'd been so stupid! It wasn't worth an argument with Anna just to win a race.

Besides, he thought, she was right. It wouldn't mean anything to win by using the shoes. *Anyone* could do it. No, he would run the race in his battered old running shoes.

As soon as he'd made up his mind, he felt much happier. He gobbled down his breakfast and rushed over to Anna's house.

When she opened the door, Jake looked his friend in the eye.

"About what I said... I'm sorry. You were right," he said quickly.

"I know. I always am!" She grinned.

Jake grinned back and then told her about his decision.

"I want to turn in those shoes before the race starts," he said. "That way, I can concentrate on my running."

The two of them dashed over to the school. No one was around yet, and it was quiet inside the school. They were hurrying along the hallway, when suddenly they noticed something was wrong. It was Jake's locker. The lock was snapped off. The door hung open, and inside there were a few notebooks and a pencil case... but no shoes.

"Where are they?" Jake cried.

That's when they realized they were not alone. A voice behind them said, "That's what *I* want to know too."

Jake and Anna whirled around. They were face-to-face with two adults – a woman and a man. Where had *they* come from?

The first thing Jake noticed was how strangely they were dressed. They were both very tall. The woman was holding something that looked like a handheld computer organizer. It let out a low beep.

The woman smiled.

At first, Jake thought it must be some kind of joke, but that wouldn't explain the strange look he saw on Anna's face...

With a jolt he realized – the man meant the future,
as in tomorrow,
    next week,
      next year,
       next...
That couldn't be – it was impossible!

Then he saw that the two adults were not so tall after all. They were just hovering in the air a few inches above the ground.

They both clicked buttons on their belts and floated gently to the floor.

Where Are the Shoes?

Anna looked calm. (Later Jake realized why: all those science-fiction books that she had read prepared her for this moment.)

"Could you please tell us what is going on?" she asked.

The little man smiled.

Mariah's with the time police. I'm an athlete, and the shoes are mine.

Jake looked at the man's potbelly. He didn't *look* much like an athlete.

In fact, Luther didn't look as if he could jog down the road without huffing and puffing. He seemed to guess what Jake was thinking.

"In our time, sports are very different," he explained to Jake and Anna. "Athletes all design and build their own special athletic equipment. For example, all running shoes have Artificial Intelligence circuits."

"What does THAT mean?" Jake asked, feeling stupid. Anna, on the other hand, understood immediately.

It means they do the running for you. They even think for themselves when they need to.

Luther nodded. He went on, "This particular pair thinks for themselves *too much* – they decided to run away. They went to a Time Travel Vacation Center and persuaded the computer there to send them back in time – to *your* time."

"That's why we're here. We need to bring the shoes home," Mariah said. "It took us a while to track them down. We were unfamiliar with your primitive methods of transportation."

She pointed to the open locker and sighed. She held up the beeping machine. Jake realized it must be for tracking the shoes.

Jake nodded grimly.

The Big Race

The four of them hurried outside.

It was almost time for the big race.
There were people everywhere, and
there was a buzz of excitement in the
air. Proud moms and dads were
picking out the best places to watch
their kids.

Runners were warming up, pinning
their numbers on their shirts, taking
last-minute advice. It wasn't hard to
spot Kevin Beadle – he was the one
with the smug look on his face. Jake
could see why. He was wearing the
smart running shoes!

Mariah nodded, but it was clear that Luther had another idea. There was a twinkle in his eye.

Mariah thought it over, then at last she agreed.

"You're going to let him run in them?" Jake asked.

Luther nodded.

For a second, Jake felt a sharp stab of jealousy. Beadle was bound to win easily with those amazing running shoes. Then he remembered his own uniform. It was almost time for the race to begin! With so much going on, he had forgotten to get changed.

After he had changed, Jake was barely in time for the start of the race.

Jake could see Kevin Beadle in the middle of the pack. A smirk played on the tall boy's face. Jake told himself to ignore it.

The whistle blew and the race began. It was five laps of the school athletic field. Right away, Kevin Beadle sprinted to the front of the pack. The shoes were doing their stuff.

Jake told himself just to concentrate on his own running. It was tough – he had spent so long running in the amazing shoes that real running was hard work.

After the first lap he was near the back, and his legs ached. He spotted Anna in the crowd. The two strange adults were still with her.

Anna shouted, "Go, Jake! You can do it!"

That made him feel better. He forced himself to go faster. Beadle, of course, was far ahead of all the other runners.

After the third lap, Jake was around the middle of the pack. His side was starting to hurt and his breath burned in his lungs, but he would not let himself slow down.

There was something good about the way it felt. Whatever happened, it was up to him, not the shoes.

Beadle increased his lead.

The fourth lap was the hardest yet. It was the time when runners began to wheeze and pant, and a lot of them slowed down. Jake just gritted his teeth and pushed on. He overtook a few runners. He didn't even look up to see how far ahead Kevin Beadle was.

Then he was passing Anna for the last time – the final lap. Even Luther and Mariah looked excited now. Luther was jumping up and down and yelling at the top of his voice.

The last lap was a blur. Jake's whole body ached – not just his legs – but on he ran.

Just when he thought he couldn't run another step, he heard a cheer from up ahead. Kevin Beadle had crossed the finish line. The tall boy was holding up his arms.

That gave Jake an extra burst of energy. He dug deep into himself and ran on for the finish line. Other runners jostled elbows against him as they made their final charge for the finish as well.

At last Jake crossed the line. He was seventh – much better than he had expected!

He bent over and tried to catch his breath. He was exhausted, but he felt really happy with himself.

He looked over at the winner, who was standing with a group of admirers. Of course, Kevin Beadle looked as fresh as he had at the start of the race.

Jake didn't even care anymore. He knew that Beadle had not really won at all. The *shoes* had won for him.

Anna rushed over and gave Jake a huge hug.

You were great!

The Shoes Get Even

Mariah and Luther came to join them. Luther slapped Jake on the back – he really seemed to like "old-fashioned" running.

"Fantastic!" he said. "I never knew running could be so exciting. It looks like very hard work, though."

"That's the whole point," Jake said. "I'm going to train really hard and next year I'm going to win this race!"

Luther and Mariah got ready to get the shoes and go home.

Wait! So why did the shoes run away to our time?

"They're a new design," Luther told them. "They even have basic emotions, but there's one problem. They're a little moody and sometimes... Well, sometimes they get angry. That's why they ran away."

The mini-computer started beeping even louder. Mariah pointed it at Kevin Beadle, who was still boasting to anyone who would listen.

She looked worried. "Yes, and we'd better hurry," she said. "According to my readings, they're getting angry right now. That boy must be irritating them. If we're not quick..."

She was too late.

One moment Beadle was bragging about how easy the race had been. Then suddenly the smirk disappeared from his face and he started jogging in place. It was clear that he couldn't stop. It was the shoes!

Then – ZOOOOOM! – Beadle took off. As he raced away, everyone could hear him screaming.

He could not stop. He jumped high over the school fence and raced along the pavement at top speed. He had no control over where the annoyed shoes were taking him.

The whole crowd at the finish line stared in silent amazement. Jake and Anna watched along with everyone else. Kevin Beadle had zipped across the road, and now he was racing toward the gas station.

It was true! Kevin Beadle sprinted through the car wash. When he came out at the other end he was soaked. A big dollop of foam perched on his head.

Still he did not stop. He didn't even slow down. He charged down the street, picking up speed, until at last he was just a small figure in the distance.

Back to Whenever

It was an hour before the running
shoes returned, bringing a stunned
Kevin Beadle with them. By that time
everyone else had gone.

"We need those shoes now," Mariah
said sternly.

Beadle didn't ask any questions. He
just pulled off the shoes and handed
them over. Then he staggered away.

Luther looked down at the shoes. Jake and Anna recognized that look in his eyes – happiness and relief, as if he had found a missing pet.

Come here, you two!

The running shoes hopped up into his arms – whatever they had been angry about was forgotten.

Mariah said, "We'd better be off. Thanks for all your help!"

It sounded as if she had a bus to catch, rather than a different time to travel to.

Luther leaned forward to Jake and spoke as one athlete to another.

The gadget in Mariah's hand beeped. Anna jumped forward.

She was too late.

The two visitors disappeared in a flash of blue light – back to *whenever* they came from.

Anna and Jake were left alone. They just looked at each other.

Well, you don't see that every day! It reminds me of this book I'm reading...

She pulled a book out of her pocket. It was called *Time Travelers of Zob*.

Jake made a face and Anna grinned. Then she pushed the book back into her pocket.

"You're right," she said. "I think I'm going to read a mystery next. I've had enough time travel for a while."

About the Author

When I was growing up in England, I always wanted to be an astronaut, a professional soccer player, or (if those didn't work out for any reason) maybe a rock star. So it came as something of a shock  when I became first a teacher and then an editor of educational books.

I have lived all over England and in Istanbul, Turkey. I'm still on the run and now live in Chicago, Illinois, with my wife and family.

I always liked cross-country running at school, and I think this story may have been a daydream of mine.

Paul Shipton